Shelley Thrasher During the 1980s

Lammy-nominated novelist, editor, and college professor Shelley Thrasher, who grew up in a small, conservative town in East Texas, was a late bloomer. Her first published poetry collection, *In and Out of Love*, chronicles personal ups and downs during the 1980s and '90s, when she came out. Most of these 160 brief, haiku-like poems feature images that speak for themselves, influenced by poets such as Allen Ginsberg and Anne Waldman, with whom she studied writing.

The first poems portray the crushes and lovers the author was involved with during this period of her life. In part two, they express the longing for something she didn't understand. Section three chronicles the painful rough spots she encountered during her journey of accepting herself as a lesbian. And the final section celebrates being in love with the woman she has now been joined with for twenty-five adventurous years.

IN AND OUT OF LOVE

IN AND OUT OF LOVE

SHELLEY THRASHER

SAPPHIRE BOOKS

SALINAS, CALIFORNIA

Book Designer - LJ Reynolds
Cover Designer - Michelle Brodeur

Sapphire Books Publishing, LLC
P.O. Box 8142
Salinas, CA 93912
www.sapphirebooks.com

Printed in the United States of America
First Edition – December 2016

This and other Sapphire Books titles can be found at
www.sapphirebooks.com

Dedication

Closing the Curtains

I don't want to close the curtains
after such a beautiful day.
But the sun has almost set.

The blue tide surges against the stone seawall,
retreats,
swells again—
on sunny days and dark nights.

Your steady surge in my life
will always keep me company.

For Cate—
my faithful, favorite poetry critic.

Cate Culpepper (1957-2014), always one of the most
enthusiastic fans of my poems, never failed to make
me laugh.

I miss you, Cate, and wish you were here to make some
witty remark about this little book.

Acknowledgments

I learned to write poetry at the Naropa Institute in Boulder, Colorado. Thank you, Allen Ginsberg, Gary Snyder, Anne Waldman, Patricia Donegan, Robert Creeley, Diane diPrima, and the other writers who taught and encouraged me to love and create Imagist poetry, as well as Kathryn Machan Aal, Patricia Schwartz, Judy Grahn, and Nancy Bereano, at a women's writing workshop near Ithaca, New York, who encouraged me to add feminism to the mix. You've all helped make coming out and expressing my real self much easier.

I'm grateful to *Bay Windows*, *ThoughtCrime*, and *Story Circle Journal* magazines for publishing early versions of some of these poems and to Barbara Zoeller for letting me use her watercolor painting on my cover.

Many thanks to all the women I've loved and lusted after, especially you, my wife Connie, for inspiring many of these poems and helping me get all of them ready for print.

Justine Saracen, who always reads and comments on whatever I write; Lee Lynch, who has supported my writing for a long time; and Chris, Schileen, and the crew at Sapphire, who make it possible to share these poems with a broader readership—I appreciate each of you.

POEMS

High
Almost
Obsession
Welcome Visit
Youth
Rebirth
Europe
Afterlove
Distraction.
April
Gamble
Transformation
Birth
Decision
Warning
Changes
Lust
Center of the World
Mirror
Longing
Learning
Taming a Runaway
Seabound
The Pond
Sea Drift
After Sonia Sanchez
Electricity
Nurture
Beside You
Flood
Sea Change
Beach Scene
Blow Your House Down
Seascape

ROUGH SPOTS

After-Course
Never Say Die
Witch Water
February
Dying Love
Autumn Friendship
Weak Growth
Coda to Lunch
Tarot Reading
Intersection
No Hope
Jealousy
Computer Love
Erosion
Anger
After a Quarrel
Scorched
Puzzle
Sea Bed
Fluidity
Silence
Fragments
Unpleasant Surprise
Dream
Switzerland
Cool
Lunch
I Just
Mt. Irazu, Costa Rica
Florida Teeth
HAPPY?

Safe
Abundance
Ephesian Artemis
Sunny Afternoon
Wet Spot
Wondering
On the Boardwalk
In the Car
Looking at You
Sappho
In-sight
Awake
Purification
Kindling
Pearl Harbor
Playing Records
The Future
Intoxication
Vortex
Relief
Deep-Sea Fishing
Tulips
Another "S"
Bonding
Goddess Worship
Making Love
Loving You
Elemental You
Baking
Breakfast
Dessert
Repose
Joy
In Texas Heat

Morning Tea
Paris
Close Contact
Constant

BEGINNINGS

Most of the poems in this book are brief. I've tried to let my images speak for themselves and to make each word count.

Hopefully, many of them will resonate with you.

The Snail

I come and go,
crawling snail-like toward the light,
rigid structure housing my jelly-like body.

Creeping forward,
I appear able to bear pain,
yet grass burrs stab, glass cuts my belly.

I inch along in silence.
Others sometimes step on me,
crack my seemingly tough shell.

Yet I keep moving
through dirt and sunlight,
leaving only a faint track.

Snail of myself,
why do you crawl?

Rage

Fire blazes

—inside—

inflamed by your

endless chitter-chatter.

Fuming, I glance at you,

yet quickly hide

behind a fake smile.

Fire rages—

destroys forests,

kills wildlife,

chars fields,

sucks streams dry.

It destroys,

flattens,

cinders my world

into ashes.

Longing

Oh, for a touch to be only a touch,

a look no larger than itself,

for the pain to burn itself out.

I want to feel the present, not the past,

let the violence of emotions wash through me,

leave me pure, sure,

able to feel each day.

Red-Hot Haiku

You are my oyster.

Stony, gray shell,

delicious cunt.

PORTRAITS OF CRUSHES AND LOVERS

First Crush

Miss Jackson wore

maroon penny-loafers,

thin white socks.

In her third-grade class,

I learned the treble-clef lines—

Every Good Boy Does Fine—

to spell *enough*.

I still hunger for

after-school cookies

she gave me at her home.

Music Teacher

She taught me

to stop,

slowly work out

difficult measures

of Chopin preludes, Bach inventions.

She made me realize,

even in small-town East Texas

people enjoy *Aida*, *Swan Lake*,

drive 200 miles to Houston

to watch them.

She cried

when we misbehaved

at choir practice:

showed me

she needed comfort.

I still called her

Mrs. Holder

the day she died.

Friday Folds, 1970

She hated to fold clothes.

She'd pile them, fresh-dried,

on the flowered sofa in her den.

From Monday through Friday morning,

she kept adding to the heap.

Jumbled blue towels with her sons' underwear—

her daughter's petticoats with the sheets—

until only a tiny space remained for us to perch,

Friday afternoons, to fold her clothes,

unfold ourselves.

We'd smooth wrinkles from dish towels,

fold sheets in an ancient dance of meeting and parting

until we civilized the percale and muslin,

tamed them to sit in her linen closet, lie on her bed.

We poured ourselves out to each other

like the water had tumbled on her clothes.

We swished through feelings, Chloroxed our thoughts.

Then, clothes dried and folded, ready for the weekend,

we knew,

though we'd heap all week,

we'd fold on Fridays.

Strength

I love the way
you row your boat.
The lake's calmness
funnels through your arms
that propel us.

I love the way
your fingers
press the keys,
pull music
from the organ's heart.

I love the way
you laugh: like a red brick
shooting skyward,
then melting
into elemental clay.

Professor's Confession

Young housewife,

broken loose for a moment,

you dash into my office—

blond-haired, blue-eyed swirl.

With purple sweatshirt

slipping down one arm,

exposing your creamy shoulder,

you make me drop my red pen.

Lover Girl

You swagger,

stride toward your old Buick,

glance back at me,

small purse flung over your shoulder—

hair out-bronzing the sun,

eyes out-greening the pines,

white-spattered black jeans

wet from our caresses.

Friday Night

In her closet
I stroke her long-sleeved,
gray-and-white striped shirt;
finger the ribbons
on the white dress
I gave her last spring
(it looked too young for me).

Then, I pick up
three pairs of clean panties
dropped on her blue bedspread,
smooth their lace,
turn them right-side out,
fold them lengthwise,
place them in her top drawer.

Lover-Daughter

I've put your picture
in each corner of my mirror
while you're away.

Top left, you smile,
your eyes the color of
leaves behind you;
sun shines on long red hair.

Top right, you still smile,
lean back against a table,
red, green, blue, yellow ribbons
braided into your vest.

Bottom left, same vest,
you study a pink flower
cradled in your strong, young fingers.
Hair swept back by wind,
face in shadow,
the landscape brown and green:
small tin shed, one lone windmill.

Lower right, sun lights wisteria leaves
behind the bench where you recline;
other leaves darken into jungle,
though one yellow daisy shines out of focus.
Your hair, most in shadow,

rests on your expressive hand,
your white face open to the sun,
chin uplifted, lips firm, eyes far-seeing.

Ex-Lover

She tried to lead,

though she couldn't

dance.

You Stood Waiting

the smell of seaweed in your hair,

coffee in your voice,

chocolate in your eyes.

I smelled my own musk,

understood

a parrot rubbing himself on his perch,

a dog humping her stuffed toy animal.

Love Lost

She lived her forty-seven-year life under a black cloud.

Her Indian mother died of cancer.

Her third husband drowned himself—

was chipped from a Colorado stream.

She drank herself unconscious,

squandered money on baubles, ignored bills,

feared a lonely old age, eating from cat-food cans.

She loved the beach though couldn't swim:

floated on a red raft, sunned, and read,

turned shells slowly in her hands.

She painted, wrote poetry,

word-waves gurgling from deep inside.

Early one morning, leaving work,

someone hit her behind her left ear.

Newspapers reported a truck ran over her,

she fell down stairs.

Now she floats on a white sheet in ICU,

drifts in a black cloud—

no brain waves.

Jane

Your eyes blue,

like the flowered curtains

in my spare room.

Your blond hair, pageboy,

makes me wish

I hadn't cut mine.

Nails short, teeth strong

like your voice,

your laugh.

You've moved me

into a new room

of my life.

Gumbo Conversation

Eyes brown

as roux

in heavy black skillet.

Hair curled

like shrimp

stirred into roux.

She combines

salt and semicolons,

okra and O'Neill.

Relaxed

Your eyes flow

mischievy to mystery

as you drift around me

in my blue room.

Contrast

I am cotton,

you—silk.

Your spider threads

drink in color more deeply,

vibrate it richly.

Fragile webwork,

strong as steel.

Softening

That damn lawn sprinkler

with its machine-gun ri-che-che-che, chi-chi-chi

wakes me again,

so I massage my tight stomach muscles,

remember my wetness

when you lick me to climax,

your brown curls

brushing the scar above my hair line.

Recall the fullness of your breasts,

like life buoys floating in the lake;

the back of your hand stroking my cheek.

I think of late afternoons coming home

in my white linen suit,

my silver bracelet clinking

against the handle of my briefcase

crammed with printouts.

Recollect your warm tears

soaking my V-necked silk blouse

when I can't turn off

my ri-che-che-che, chi-chi-chi.

Changing

Your brown eyes

lick me like puppies' tongues.

How quickly they flicker

from cool Norway

to warm Spain.

Strange Music

We float somewhere in the wide white space

between bass and treble clefs.

No black lines to cling to,

no bounded space to live in,

no sharps or flats

to tell us how to sound.

Your brown eyes my notes,

your fingers my only lines.

Peeling Summer Peaches

Lounging in my backyard under an oak tree,

peeling perfumed peaches from my sister's lavish trees,

I swim to Lake Michigan, on your postcard.

You say you miss me, sign with "Love."

Peach skin clings as tightly to its sweet meat

as we did when swaying on the dance floor,

music wrapped around us like a sheet of silken clouds.

Peach skin—

you rub lotion around my bikini bottom again,

touch me

like a mother soothes a headache,

a sister cures a heartache,

a lover strokes a thigh.

My knife slides quietly,

skins spiral to the ground—

juice seeps down my wrist.

Licking my arm,

I taste your lips

again.

LONGING

Phone Call

Your voice rises,

crying like a seagull's,

when you hear mine on the line.

I sit straighter;

your words flood me—

bathe, stroke, refresh

till I'm swimming

in my mother's womb.

I've a catch

under my green turtleneck,

under the zipper

of my jeans.

Love-40

After a month apart,

we whiz our words past each other,

bounce them off my apartment walls.

Lifeless, they plop to the green carpet.

We serve again, rapid-fire,

still can't rally

till I touch your arm.

High

You're a mountain,

covered with chartreuse grass.

I long to wander on your slopes,

pick brilliant wildflowers.

Almost

We stand tall at the edge of the campus.

Your green eyes pull me.

But we both blink,

turn,

return.

Obsession

You magnetize me:

a young girl up-fingers her yoyo;

the Queen Mary winds in her anchor.

Welcome Visit

You glide into my room—

tall and lean,

long black-and-white robe,

hair towel-turbaned,

holding my poem.

You sit on my narrow bed,

I close beside you.

As we discuss my work,

the words blur.

Youth

I long into your lime-lemon eyes;

my past explodes.

Old scars melt,

become smooth as your cheek.

Rebirth

Silver chrysalis cracks—

peony bud unfurls—

green pine tiptoes toward the sun.

Europe

I used to be Poland:
armies invaded at will,
bloody corpses,
charred barns on green plains.

I tried to be Switzerland:
trains like clockwork,
mothering mountains,
cows munching clover.

But I've settled for France:
graveyards with white crosses,
ballet schools in each village,
late-night talks in cafés.

Afterlove

From toes to tongue

I tingle—

your Botticelli body.

Distraction

Your celery eyes

peek at me between

words of Steinbeck's "The Chrysanthemums."

Their upward slant

lures me from essays, red pen—

makes me sit, head on hand,

write, not read.

April

Thoughts of you

bathe my sun-baked body,

cool the breeze.

Gamble

I've put

all my eggs

in your basket.

Please,

don't break them.

Transformation

You've sparked my red-brick heart.

You make me

lose my glaze, return to clay.

Birth

I struggle

to be born

from safe inside myself.

Claw the walls

of my womb—

avoid the light.

Am I a monster—

eight-fingered,

three heads?

Will my birth cries

split ears,

repulse delivering hands?

Decision

On the highway

stood a huge roadblock:

LESBIANS AHEAD. NO TRAFFIC.

I always turned around, drove off.

What type of landscape lay ahead?

Friends, family, terrified,

didn't notice, acknowledge the sign.

I drove up at night,

shone my headlights.

Finally, tired of restrictions,

I pushed the roadblock aside,

traveled on.

Warning

Beware

the guilt

dealer.

Changes

Spring-young in East Texas,

I despised stinky, dainty,

purple-blooming chinaberry trees.

Summer,

we used their hard, green fruit

as slingshot ammo—

bruised each other's flesh.

Fall, in Austin,

I noticed chinaberries:

lynx-eye yellow, English-pea round.

Each fruit tipped a long, straw-like stem,

joined to a branch like a finger to a hand.

Sister of the mahogany tree,

a chinaberry sheltered the patio

of my first gay bar.

Lust

squeezes my breasts,

twists my stomach,

weakens feet and legs,

arms and shoulders—

forces my brain

to think

only of you.

Center of the World

Suddenly,

you are the steel rod

my pink-and-blue globe

spins around.

Mirror

My gold-burst green eyes

gaze back at me—

full of you.

Longing

I need

your fertile hands

on my body

as long as

arid soil craves rain,

the bluebonnet is blue,

the Gulf's waves never cease.

Learning

Unable to swim,

we paddle one stroke,

grab one another,

drag into darkness.

Back to our familiar logs—

(we wanted to leave them)—

we clutch their rough bark,

rest, store our strength

for another plunge.

Taming a Runaway

The waves inside me

begin to gallop,

pant so loudly

I hear only foaming questions.

You soothe my bucking sea

with a few gentle strokes.

Seabound

Let's swim far out to sea.

Match stroke to stroke,

arch over gentle waves,

laugh when salt fills our mouths,

let mother-water support us,

become as strong as our wombs.

Then, exhausted,

lie side by side

while our sun fills us

with strength.

The Pond

Emerge,

slowly,

from the black pond,

where gray weeds entangle,

mud-sucked for too long.

Sea Drift

Our weekend conversation

washed me into a turquoise sea.

I float in a gold cup,

eat grapes and bananas,

let drifting pieces of ourselves

merge and coalesce

to birth

a new Venus.

After Sonia Sanchez

Returning home, I listen to our three days in the waves,

play them again and again,

scatter myself among your blue eyes and brown bathing suit.

Our openness plays from my records.

I can hear our mothers singing.

Electricity

My eyes blink

LUST—LUST—LUST—

like a ceaseless neon sign,

every time I glance at you.

Nurture

Milk-fed, my black kitten

quiets her mews,

starts to purr,

wants to rub against your leg.

Beside You

On the warm sand,

waves' rhythms pulsing with our own,

I begin to thaw.

Trickles of melting snow

flake into drop,

collect as slowly as diamonds grow.

Finally overflowing their riverbank,

they soak parched earth,

rouse green palm trees from beige sand.

Flood

It rained forty-two years.

Behind the brick wall,

growing higher and thicker,

water collected drop by splash,

hollowed out a great fluid-filled cavern.

Pressure mounted,

washed out bricks,

left chinks for trickles.

Now the wall's so weak,

pressure so strong,

all farmland around

will surely be flooded.

Sea Change

You've unmoored me

into life's flow.

Tied at the dock,

I've barnacled,

cabin damp and molding,

sails rotting.

Your fresh breeze

moves me

toward the ocean's spray.

Beach Scene

Two white shrimp boats glide

geese-like on a turquoise pond.

Two white gulls struggle against the wind,

then turn and relax in its power.

Two smooth shells snuggle

in pink and blue sand.

Blow Your House Down

The noisy Gulf puffs, huffs

against our orange nylon tent.

We curl like shrimp

on sleeping bags and makeshift pillows.

Outside the half-oval screen,

mosquitoes whine and stab.

Above, the upright Big Dipper

points toward the North Star.

Seascape

In the waves of the Gulf,

you bob like a child,

cling to my hand

in fear of the sea.

In the wash of my sea,

I toss like a child,

learn from your hands

not to fear myself so.

ROUGH SPOTS

After-Course

"What is this magic spell you've cast over me?"

"Sex," she said.

"Pure and simple?"

"Pure, at least," she said.

"But not simple."

Never Say Die

Like Wile E. Coyote in Saturday-morning Road Runner
cartoons,

I pop back into round

after you flatten me with instant opinions:

"You're not living in the real world."

"You're weird."

Witch Water

Jade fluid,

lake water,

seduces,

retreats.

Bright sunlight,

warm surface,

large carp swims,

cold depths.

February

One hyacinth blooms pink

within her sunlit circle of stones.

Among distant weeds,

under a dead oak,

a lone palmetto blade

pulsates

in the cold wind.

Dying Love

All summer, we bodysurfed together,

hunted sand dollars,

drank beer,

talked for hours.

Now you wear long pants,

I, still in shorts.

Sitting on a flat rock at the beach's edge,

sand blowing around us,

we miss more than meet,

jar more than jell.

Autumn winds kick up surf,

the air chills, and rain falls.

Autumn Friendship

Edge of the gray Gulf,

we sit in low, plastic-webbed chairs,

watch the setting sun.

The sea gnaws at the beach;

our chair legs sink in wet sand.

Your beautiful tanned face,

lined by our time in the sun,

tenses

as your husband

calls your name.

I freeze at the sound.

Fog rolls in, chills the breeze.

Soft rain makes us shiver.

We fold our chairs,

head for your cabin.

Mosquitoes begin to whine.

The sea's strong current

rushes diagonally toward the beach.

Last week the undertow

ingested two people.

Weak Growth

My love for you shot up

like a pine in a crowded forest:

tall, thin trunk,

few branches to shade us.

Now the pine-bark beetles

have attacked.

Coda to Lunch

After you've come and gone,

your words, phrases resonate

until they swell into a symphony,

vibrating my mind

till long after dark.

I replay our canon

until the needle gathers lint,

the record grows scratchy.

Tarot Reading

Sitting on my brown shag carpet,

we let our shoulders touch, our arms caress—

examine the Queen of Swords,

who holds a face.

You: "That's my mask.

I've been stripping it away

since we last made love."

Your straight black hair

does frame an honest face,

even more beautiful than your painted, bewitching one

twelve years ago.

I slide into your eyes, wells of black energy.

Your lips attract.

But I deny the pull to kiss their narrow pinkness,

remember how I've savored your entire smooth body,

except them.

Intersection

On a dark side street,

stopped behind a car with embracing lovers,

I lean over,

finally kiss you.

Lips, teeth, pressure to move on—

we drive to a main street.

No Hope

At Koto's of Japan,

you pick up our shredded past with chopsticks,

drip tears into your red wine,

carry home five shrimp tempura

in a white cardboard box

to your husband.

Jealousy

When you point your hose

at her instead of me,

my pansies wilt, shrivel.

Computer Love

Just thinking of losing you

I feel off-line—

an O.E.I. Business Form

tractor-feeding quietly

page by page,

line by line,

printless.

Erosion

Like a mouse

nibbling cheese,

you gnaw me away.

Anger

She spews words

like hot grease bubbling

over the side of a skillet.

They hit the gas flame,

almost extinguish it;

contaminate the kitchen air;

blacken the pan.

After a Quarrel

I sprawl, nude,

arms outstretched,

on the bed.

She huddles on the other side,

under a white sheet.

August heat, humidity

press us

like dogwood blossoms under glass.

Four-bladed ceiling fan

cuts the air,

throws it toward us.

I turn toward her,

embrace her curled back.

My breasts, her buttocks

begin to round out

like rose petals opening.

But I pull away,

feel only the fan's breeze.

Scorched

The drought persists.

My once-green-grass heart

a fistful of sere brown blades.

Puzzle

When a woman is hurting,

do you lick up her pain,

like a cat at her saucer?

Do you rub it away,

like stroking a lion?

Endure its roar,

refuse fingers in ears?

Look in its face,

brave its yellow glare?

Sea Bed

Living together,

I grasped our bed's shore—

she splashed in its sea.

I, in barnacle-ball—

she, in octopus-spread.

Now I lose my shell, grow fins,

float instead of cling;

enter her waters;

expand like a blowfish

ripe with poison.

Fluidity

You were Venus,

melting into each wave,

succumbing to its power—

rebirthing on shore.

You flicked your love around me,

encouraged Poseidon

to rouse his roaring, lulling

swell in me.

Now you both have shipwrecked me,

left only ruined shells.

Silence

As passion ebbs and pain subsides,

silence covers us like sand.

We struggle to brush off

this grit, but

it settles in cuts not yet healed.

Irritated by grains like ground diamonds,

we douse it with sea water,

half-hoping to grow new gems.

But its cool hardness

clings, spreads.

Fragments

Broken into four pieces,

the barnacle ball I

found on the beach hides

in the pocket of my

white leather purse.

I try to fit the fragments

into a round shape again

but soon give up.

Their bony whiteness—

dry in my hand.

Unpleasant Surprise

Returning home, I discover

dog shit

on my blue hyacinths.

Dream

Plodding

across the Sahara

on my camel

for days—

jolted,

sore,

thirsty—

no oasis in view—

I try to remember

the Mediterranean.

Switzerland

We stroll beside a glacier stream,

eat ham, black-red cherries,

spit hard pits into icy, hurried water.

You spread butter, cheese on brown bread.

I gather yellow, blue, red meadow-flowers.

Back at the hotel, I'm dizzy.

You offer tea and croissants.

I rest while you shop.

You buy red Swiss-army knives

for your husband, your son.

Later, in dim café:

You: "I'm concerned. Is Nancy a lesbian?"

Me: "No. Not really. Just tired of men."

You: "Be careful. You're not, are you?"

Me: "I'm not sure. Maybe."

The next day,

on hard, upright train benches.

You: "You're a leaner.

Your constant self-analysis bores me."

Me: "My head hurts."

Cool

You sound as cold as Lake Michigan.

What happened

to Florida's warm, salty waves?

Lunch

The black olives

in my Greek salad—

bitter.

I Just

want to ask you:

what makes you think

you have a right

to all my free time?

Mt. Irazu, Costa Rica

Alone on the edge,

hair-curling cold fog,

I stare into gray-black emptiness.

Red lava once cascaded here.

Its ashes forced people to wear masks.

Cattle, tobacco fields smothered in its residue.

Now leafy plants, animals flourish.

And on Irazu's barren heights

lie treasures of cooled flowing fire.

Florida Teeth

The garbage disposal

grabs for my middle finger,

its six-slit mouth black.

I offer it cantaloupe rinds to chomp.

It rests, placated,

still as malevolent as an alligator.

HAPPY?

How many new people

And books to read.

Perhaps I'll

Pry myself away from

You.

Breaking

She cracked my crystal pitcher,

bought in Yugoslavia,

carried home on my lap.

She used hot water to rinse it,

lemonade cold—

ping!

Liquid now oozes through.

She cracked my K-Mart teapot,

its glass like a soap bubble.

She boiled water into steam;

the pot's fragments

caught in the electric coils.

Broken wineglasses

slipping through her hands—

chips on antique vases,

nicks in china cups.

Everything fragile shatters

all around us.

April Memories

"APRIL IS THE CRUELEST MONTH...

STIRRING DULL ROOTS WITH SPRING RAIN."

I've just scooped out the ashes

from our last fire,

when we lay on my grandmother's quilt,

blazed together.

"APRIL SHOWERS BRING MAY FLOWERS."

I've vacuumed my fireplace,

filled it with a wooden bowl of potpourri

topped with dried purple statice and red roses

from my last-April lover.

"WHAN THAT APRILL WITH HIS SHOURES SOOTE

THE DROGHTE OF MARCH HATH PERCED TO THE ROOTE..."

I've torn crawfish mounds from my soggy yard,

filled the ruts the wrecker left

the night you backed into my ditch,

then never came again.

Disillusioned

Like my five Yugoslavian crystal wineglasses,

knocked off my window shelves

when I jerked up the panes,

I lie shattered

on my red-brick floor.

Bruised

My purple heart,

a boxing bag

battered by your bare fists.

After a Fight

The dry scent of ashes

spreads throughout the house.

A blackened log,

burned in two,

sprawls on a rusty grate

above gray residue.

Paris, 1983

Saturday night in Paris—

Malakof's Restaurant, Trocadero Metro.

Greg shoves you: "Scoot over, woman."

You smile, brown eyes like burnt holes in a saddle
blanket,

pull blue package of Gitanes from your expensive
leather purse—

though you don't smoke.

He jerks to attention.

Crack of a sparking match. "Let's double-drag," he
says.

Heads together, you share fire and smoke.

Carelessly, he tosses green match folder to me.

I order salad Nicoise, veal escalope—

he, escargot and pepper steak.

You the same as he.

I choose our demi-liter of red wine.

Then I retreat to Texas.

Stop by Nancy's, who feeds me biscuits and milk.

From Texas I wander to a country of solitude,

distantly hear you say, "She certainly isn't any fun tonight."

He says, "Some guys can drink a case of beer and not be that far gone."

He holds my arm stiffly, carefully,

leads me down, through, and up the Metro stops:

Villiers, La Fourche, Brochant.

You never touch me.

He tells you, "It's good I was with y'all tonight.

You couldn't handle her by yourself."

In Hotel Berthier, room 7120,

you say, "Get undressed."

I don't move,

want you to mother me.

You don't.

After you're asleep,

I let leather sandals drop, loudly,

pull out white-stone earrings,

shower slowly.

The next morning.

You: "You seemed exhausted last night,

so dopey I was afraid

someone would jump us in the Metro.

Greg's certainly mature for nineteen, don't you think?"

Me: "I don't think any of us are."

Attacked

You chopped off my fingers,

then cursed me

because I bled

on your white carpet.

Friend-ache

Bone-deep ache in my hip, almost pleasant—
you will be gone when I return.

A stranger in your house,
behind your desk.

You will take from me
the scent of cinnamon and grapes,
snapping brown eyes,
Persephone, Athena, Aphrodite.

The ache persists—
neither hot bath nor heating pad
can relax it—
so deep
my lover's massage can't soothe it.

Last Lunch

Your new apartment,

crammed with the sagging bed we once shared,

strange furniture all your own.

I bring traditional Sunday lunch: roast, potatoes—the
works.

You welcome me—

I, eventually, at ease,

wash familiar brown pottery,

wipe greasy cabinet,

find your poem to her.

It details her strengths—

you once detailed mine.

I start to burn poem

but turn fire inward,

pretend not to see words

obviously in view.

Your probing tongue makes a parting intrusion.

By the way,

your kisses always repulsed me.

California

While digging,

I struck pain.

No gold rush.

Relief

Slivers of crystalized pain

work their way

to the surface of the wound.

To Anne, With Thanks

"What do you do with the pain?"
I remember asking you.
I don't recall your answer—
only your sympathy—
the most valuable gift you could give.

I had to find my own way:
I've talked it out,
stalked it out,
written it out,
bitten it out,
played it out,
made it out,
chewed it out,
screwed it out,
screamed it out,
dreamed it out,
taught it out,
fought it out.

.

I've drunk it out,
punked it out,
duked it out,
puked it out,
thrown it out,
groaned it out,
even boomed it out,

assumed it out,
shot it out,
got it out.

Then,
at bedrock,
I cried it out.

Note. I usually stick to short, Imagist poems, but once in a while the influence of Anne Waldman, one of my mentors at Naropa, slips through and out comes a poem like this and the next one. And I do use rhyme occasionally, like I did in the poem you just read. It's fun.

When

When a skillet burns,

I drop it.

When a horsefly bites,

I brush it.

When a skeeter sucks,

I slap it.

When a roach appears,

I crush it.

When a chigger clings,

I yank it.

When a whiner gripes,

I lop her.

When an old friend grates,

I cut her.

When a lover's late,

I drop her.

Camelot's Dissolving

chill wind

mouses through cracks,

around giant oak door—

the sun forsakes its power

though spring tiptoes near—

flowers fade,

droop

You Left

the butts of More cigarettes,

the smell of White Shoulders,

a quart jar stained with tea,

two lemon hulls,

a blue tennis shoe,

an unpaid phone bill.

Wanting You

My body aches,

my throat chokes,

my lips dry.

How can I endure your absence?

Grief

Being drawn and quartered,

I have to stop the horses

from pulling me to pieces,

from yanking me apart.

After So Long

you returned—

a melodious voice from my past.

You opened a new door,

led us up a staircase—

almost to the top—

played the irresistible music

of your fantasies

until I believed them.

Now the loss of you, again—

unbearable.

Gone

You fed me

tabouli and biscuits,

endless talk on the phone.

No more.

SAD

Since you left

And I'm still here,

Do write.

Underwater

When I start to swim,

an octopus grabs my ankle,

grasps my wrist,

circles my waist,

pulls me down—

covers me with

its mud-black ink.

Backyard

In each gash

the armadillo left

while clawing for worms,

I'm planting

a sprig

of San Augustine grass.

Rebuilding

The lumber of my life

lies splintered around my feet.

Another damn hurricane has hit, left

a broken beam of betrayed friendship here,

a cracked joist like a temper tantrum there.

Remnants of yellow paint recall happier days.

I'll discard rotten oak,

salvage straight, true pine,

straighten bent nails,

add new paint,

rebuild

a lovelier home.

IN LOVE

Debut

You've been standing on the stage of my mind

all summer.

You've moved forward,

spoken a few lines,

retreated among the other actors.

When the spotlight has hit you,

I've shifted it quickly,

afraid of your reluctance

to follow the script.

Now you're center stage,

floodlights making you radiant.

When I close my eyes,

I see only you.

Sunday Afternoon

Words swim

between us

like goldfish in a bowl.

New Life

You've hacked a trail

through pine woods 'round my house.

You've pounded my door

till I've opened.

You've brought warm red wine

that sparkles, entrances,

like your eyes,

your tongue,

your mind.

Spring

Sweet, cold water

bubbled from the spring deep underground.

Schoolchildren drank from it,

slid down pine-needle hills,

shared the spring's cool secret

giggling out of white sand,

green ferns waving.

Molded-leaf years,

withered fern,

dead pine branches

clogged its whispers—

turned fountain to swamp.

You rake my rotten past,

unveil my pure sand.

Water sparkles out,

crisps the leaves

of my drooping violets.

Options

Instead of a car, give me revenge—

it'll get me there.

An electric stove—it's not so great—

hate burns more fiercely by far.

And a new winter coat—think I need one?

I prefer your cuddly love.

The TV set's never turned on—

you do that instead.

Chocolate candy, ice cream, pie—

your breasts beat them by a mile.

Central air/central heat can't cool or warm

as well as your shrug or your smile.

Protection

You are the black leather boots

I wear to walk

among snakes.

Animal Trainer

You pet the hellhounds

clawing at my legs,

drooling down my neck—

transform them

into cavorting puppies.

Blooming

My pale-blue flower

on its grassy stem

shrinks, stunned like a pansy

after a freeze.

You shine,

its blue petals open,

reveal its golden center.

Safe

Like a babe in the womb,

an orange in its skin,

a snail in its shell.

Abundance

The joy you give me:

a whale in a pond,

a jet in a backyard,

an eagle at a bird feeder,

Sappho in poetry,

Mona Lisa in art,

Billie Jean King.

Ephesian Artemis

Standing marble-still in Kusadasi's small museum,
against dark brick wall, festooned with ivy,
honeybees, flowers, lions, cattle
decorate her torso, arms, headpiece.
A garland hangs above her thirteen breasts;
hands reach out, lack fingers.
Mouth and eyes smile, noseless.

Cruise-ship tourists shuffle past,
point at her many breasts, snicker.
Their yellow bus rumbles past
a lone sign pointing out her temple:

ARTEMISIUM.

A seven-ancient-world's wonder,
its lone pillar stands in water pool,
resembles checkers stacked by the child of a goddess.
Remnants of church, mosque, fort
loom in the background.

She stands derided, neglected in Turkey
but thrives between my Texas sheets.
Her warm breasts feed me.

When we talk, her voice sounds
strong as a lion's roar,
soft as a flower.
I taste her honey.

Sunny Afternoon

Spanish moss,

cypress knees—

your fingers caress my wrist.

Wet Spot

Holding hands

in the park with you.

My black satin slip—

soaked.

Wondering

Your eyes lively as squirrels,

your skin smooth as magnolias,

your lips—?

On the Boardwalk

We lean against the rail.

You face the bayou,

I, the lake.

Bellies brush—

December sun shines, hot.

In the Car

When you gaze at me that way,

I don't hear the traffic,

have to glance away.

Looking at You

Slavic cheekbones,

Oriental eyes

mesmerize.

Sappho

Standing in the ring of Mytilene's harbor,

famous Lesbian poet smiles on her pedestal,

lyre in hand.

Ringed by swaying pines,

you talk to me—

I hear her sing.

In-sight

When I close my eyes

I see

your face.

Awake

I didn't sleep last night.

Your face, starlit,

kept me awake.

Purification

I'm using Lizst and Chopin

to scrub the brown grime

from my bathtub,

anticipating your clean, warm water.

Kindling

Your pine

fires

my oak.

Pearl Harbor

Fifty years ago today,

bombs shattered.

Tonight, we heal.

Playing Records

Old love songs spin.

We, on a purple satin comforter,

kiss the past into the future.

The Future

In twenty years, who knows?

I do know, now—

I crave your body close to mine.

Intoxication

You fall—I rise

to greet your touch.

The taste of white wine.

Vortex

Caught in a tornado of rose petals—

sucked higher, higher,

to Munchkin Land,

I swirl from black-and-white

to color.

Relief

All my smothered kisses—

strangled caresses—

aborted endearments—

I give to you.

Deep-Sea Fishing

I bend, throw lines

into your white waves.

You move beneath me—

surging,

salty,

sighing—

yield

oceanic delicacies.

Tulips

We unfold to each other,

the sun, the stars—

petal on petal

of heart-red softness.

What a glorious renaissance.

Another "S"

I invited you

for spaghetti and Scrabble.

Love our game change.

Bonding

We talked around the clock,

with lips, tongues,

hands, bodies.

Goddess Worship

The Great Goddess—

revered, adored for 50,000 years.

Last night, sucking your breasts,

I rediscovered religion.

Making Love

Your rose-petal hands

move, tease, caress—

make me bloom.

Loving You

Finally, I understand

the lyrics

of old love songs.

Elemental You

Rain on my camellias,

wind that stirs my chimes,

earth to ground my restless pace,

blaze to warm my mind.

Baking

Your blueberry-muffin breath

turns on my oven,

heats it to 450 degrees:

ready for baking.

Breakfast

We crack passion's eggs—

fry them white by white in hot grease,

scramble them in slick butter.

Dessert

To make great pecan pie,

use Karo syrup,

plenty of nuts,

long, slow heat.

Repose

I lie quietly

in a warm, rose-scented bath,

thinking of you.

Joy

My heart's a huge washtub

of hot, sudsy water

that keeps overflowing.

In Texas Heat

I fill an empty quart jar

with ice cubes,

1/4 cup sugar,

1/2 Sunkist lemon,

Lipton tea.

As I stir with my ice-teaspoon,

some liquid sloshes

down the side of my jar.

Morning Tea

I will bring

you my love

in a flowered china cup.

Otherwise,

I'd drown you.

Paris

Divorced, I fled to Paris.

Mona Lisa smirked,

Venus de Milo stood armless,

the Eiffel Tower loomed.

Separated, I escaped to Paris.

Winged Victory stood headless,

Rodin's Lovers pulsed with passion,

cars sped around the Arc de Triomphe.

Infatuated, I rushed through Paris.

Mona flirted,

Venus allured,

the Eiffel Tower promised new heights.

Loved, I explored Paris.

Mona smiled,

Winged Victory offered shelter,

the Arc de Triomphe framed the City of Love.

Close Contact

I'm a rock.

You—a dragonfly—

always touch down,

never fly far away.

Constant

Like the tide,

I swell and shrink—

you, my moon.

About the Author

Shelley Thrasher, professor emerita of English, began writing poetry in the 1970s. In the early '80s, she spent two summers at the Naropa Institute in Boulder, Colorado, where she studied under poets Allen Ginsberg, Robert Creeley, Gary Snyder, Anne Waldman, Pat Donegan, and Diane di Prima. In the mid-'80s, she attended the Feminist Women Writers Workshop near Ithaca, New York, where she studied with Judy Grahn and other talented women. She's been writing and publishing poetry ever since, when the mood strikes her.

Shelley has been an editor of LGBT fiction since 2004 and has published three novels: *The Storm* (2012), *First Tango in Paris* (2014), and *Autumn Spring* (2015), which was a Lambda Literary finalist in the Lesbian Romance category. She's currently writing a memoir.

A native Texan, she has traveled the world and lives in East Texas with her wife Connie, their two dogs, cat, and parrot. She enjoys working in the yard, traveling, and socializing with members of the LGBT community.